Magic Whispers

by

Alina Kotmina

Foreword by Atticus

If you have any questions about Alina's story or would like to
share your journey, please send us an email to
akmagicwhispers@gmail.com and follow Alina's writing
Instagram @_keep_writing.

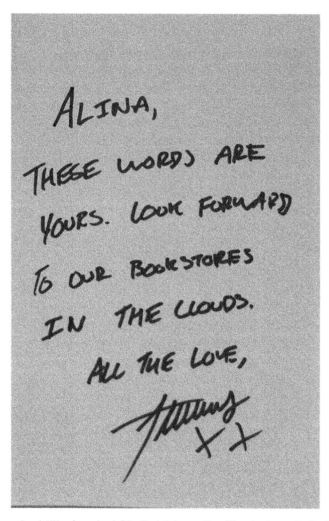

ALINA,

THESE WORDS ARE YOURS. LOOK FORWARD TO OUR BOOKSTORES IN THE CLOUDS.

ALL THE LOVE,

XX

Alina pre-ordered Atticus' new book "The Dark Between Stars." It arrived a week after Alina passed. Afterward, her family traveled to New York with the unopened package to attend one of Atticus' book signings. Atticus asked if he could keep this copy to remember Alina forever. Her family said yes.

Foreword

I remember being in Alina's hospice room; she was unconscious, surrounded by friends and family. I was reading some of her poems to her from a book her mother gave me. I came to one of the last poems in the journal. It was about a boy and how she got goosebumps on her arm whenever he touched her. At that moment, her mother looked down at Alina's arm: "Look," she said, "Goosebumps." Alina opened her eyes and looked around the room and then closed her eyes for the last time. She passed away a few moments later. I only knew Alina for a moment, but she had a monumental impact on my life. I'm so thankful to have known a glimpse of her and feel forever intertwined. I look forward to the day we can drink coffee and explore bookstores in the clouds. Until then, I'll cherish the memory of her and these beautiful words she left behind.

xx

ATTICUS

From left to right: Mom Irina, Atticus, sister Zlata, and friend Laura
at Atticus' book signing in New York on September 9, 2018.

About The Author

"This may be a sad chapter but you are not a sad story."
—Unknown

This quote is now forever engraved on the Facebook profile of Alina Kotmina, and we couldn't think of a more appropriate quote for all to remember her by.

The last year of Alina's life was a sad chapter in an otherwise happy story. Even in that last year, Alina was full of life, traveling when she could, writing the brilliant poems in the coming pages, losing herself in music, making those around her laugh for hours on end and dancing... always dancing.

She had a way of making people feel special like she was the lucky one to know YOU, but we knew WE were the lucky ones all along. From her hugs that could end wars to her smile that could light up a room, she left a lasting impression on everyone who crossed paths with her. We hope her poetry leaves a lasting impression on you as well.

Remember: Alina's chapter may have ended sadly, but the truth is we all have the ability to write a happy story for ourselves. We all deserve it. Now go out and make some magic. Tell them Alina sent you.

BLANK PAGES

Alina loved to live in the words written by others. As a way to intertwine your story with her story, we have left blank pages throughout the book for you to write whatever comes to mind: a poem, a short story, or even a drawing.

As a true millennial, Alina also loved social media and spent hours looking at inspirational quotes and poems. To pay tribute to her, post your creation on Instagram and use the hashtag #MagicforAlina so we can see how she inspired the world through her words.

Alina's birth place, Petrozavodsk, Russia.

Does he know your favorite color?

Does he know how you like your coffee?

Does he know your favorite song?

Does he know what book you are reading?

Does he know your birthday?

Does he know your favorite number?

Does he know your dreams for the future?

Does he.....

A.K.

She craved freedom

  Like a caged animal

Trapped inside her insecurities.

A.K.

Alina and one of her beloved tattoos: "She's mad but she's Magic…"

She's a rare vision

Crazy beautiful disaster

She's not for everyone

She's a slave and a master

She's an angel in disguise

Or a devil play pretend

She's like unicorn – unique

She's a lover and a friend.

A.K.

Notes on Self-Relection

Write a poem, a short story, or draw what self-reflection means to you. Tag @_keep_writing on Instagram and use the hashtags, #MagicForAlina and #SelfReflection

Step one

    Open your heart

Step two

    Open your eyes.

A.K.

The right person will find you

And they will never leave

Patience, my love.

A.K.

Alina was inspired by lighthouses; she loved the romantic feelingthat they portrayed. Her family honored her love for lighthousesby spreading her ashes at the lighthouse in Saint-Tropez, France.

I'll be the light to bring you home
Your own lighthouse on the horizon
I'll shine bright all through the night
To keep you safe in starlight.

A.K.

Notes on Travel

Write a poem, a short story, or even draw your favorite travel destination. Tag @_keep_writing on Instagram and use the hashtags #MagicForAlina and #Traveling

Love is messy

Love is wild

Love is free

Love is worthwhile.

A.K.

Located in her hometown Petrozavodsk, Russia, this dreamy path was one of Alina's favorite walks to take in.

When time is right
Our paths will cross
For the last time
For a lifetime.

A.K.

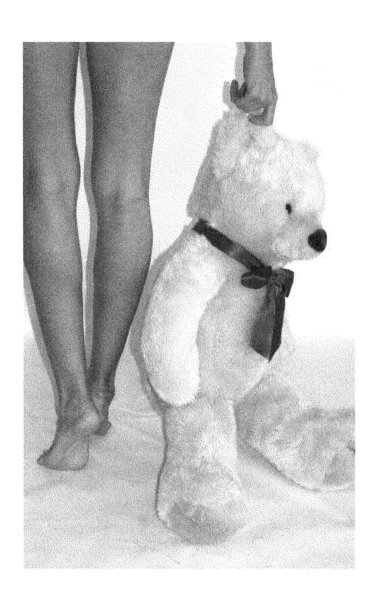

During your struggle

p l e a s e,

don't lose yourself

we all have some trouble

finding self-love and hope as well.

A.K.

Notes on Life Struggles

Write a poem, a short story, or even draw your current life struggles. Tag @_keep_writing on Instagram and use hashtags #MagicForAlina and #LifeStruggles

34

Your love was just for show

A part of entertainment

I would have applauded

But I was too busy

Gathering pieces of my broken heart.

A.K.

Alina's family, mom and sister, mourning her passing during the life celebration ceremony on the beach in Palm Beach, Florida.

There are times when you are weak
          You wait for a phone call, for a text
          For a glance, for a touch, for a kiss
The things you crave, the things you miss.

A.K.

He found her

When she was abandoned

Lost and confused

And simply mishandled

He took her pain

And made it his

To free her heart

AND NOW IT SINGS.

A.K.

Alina had the most beautiful eyes.

When you look into my eyes

    Do you see a bottomless ocean?
Or clear sunny skies

    A summer thunderstorm
Or frosty winter ice.

A.K.

Notes on Self Love

Write a poem, a short story, or even draw your self-portrait.
Tag @_keep_writing on Instagram and use the hashtags #Magic-
ForAlina and #SelfLove

She watched his life from far away,

    Like a mermaid who's not able to walk

In his world.

A.K.

She felt her pillow move and then a gentle kiss

On the tip of her nose, her lips

Stretched in a happy smile,

and then his lips were on hers

"Good morning," he whispered.

A.K.

Put your arms around me

    Keep me safe and warm

I'll put my arms around you

    Let's stand like this listening to the storm.

A.K.

I don't want perfection

I want happiness.

A.K.

Notes on Your Happy Place

Write a poem, a short story, or even draw your happy place. Tag @_keep_writing on Instagram and use the hashtags #MagicForAlina and #MyHappyPlace

Alina's favorite drink was coffee. This photo was taken in Savannah, Georgia, on her last trip before she could physically travel no more.

The smell of coffee teased her nostrils

    She breathed in deeply still half asleep

He took her hand and kissed her every finger,

    Then the wrist... He kept going up

The whole arm, she was completely awake

    By the time he reached her shoulder

He lingered at her neck while she waited in

    In anticipation, finally his lips touched her lips

He tasted like coffee – delicious and enticing

    "Good morning," he whispered.

A.K.

Alina and her friend Jennie collaborated on this illustration.

She's here, you're there
The Universe is in between

Please, be aware
Of everything that could've been...

A.K.

Alina and her furry babies Leia and Khalee.

If I can't be myself
Then what's the point?

A.K.

Notes on Your True Self

Write a poem, a short story, or even draw what the words true self means to you. Think about it, what makes you YOU? Tag @_keep_writing on Instagram and use the hashtags #MagicForAlina and #MyTrueSelf

The butterfly is used by many hospices worldwide as a symbol representing life and spirit. At Alina's hospice, a butterfly on the patient's door symbolized the passing away of a patient.

She battles the pain

  Day after day

True warrior at heart

  Because there is no other way.

A.K.

The three musketeers, Alina, her mom and sister, holding hands, no matter what. This moment was captured at Alina's hospice in Jupiter, Florida.

There are no instructions

on how to love

You either do or you don't.

A.K.

Notes on Love

Write a poem, a short story, or even draw what love means to you. Tag @_keep_writing on Instagram and use the hashtags #MagicForAlina and #Love

This is the last photoshoot that Alina and her mom did together before Alina lost her hair due to chemo treatments.

She was born way too sensitive
for this unkind world.

A.K.

Breathe in faith

    Breathe out fear.

             A.K.

Notes on thr Unexplainable

Write a poem, a short story, or even draw what unexplainable means to you. Tag @_keep_writing on Instagram and use the hashtags #MagicForAlina and #TheUnexplainable

I cannot write a song
But I can always sing along
A melody will flow through me
Lyric forever in my memory.

A.K.

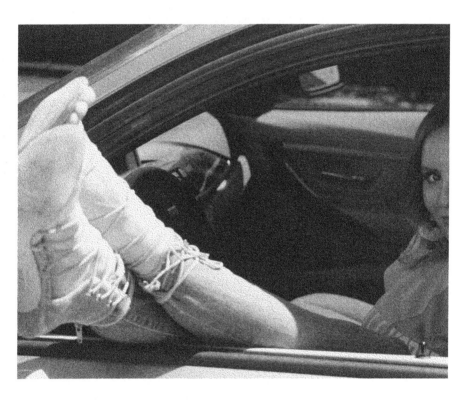

Remember that time in the parking garage,

    You were standing next to your car

While I was walking from the other side

    I watched you casually lean on your red mustang

Waiting for me, your body at ease

    While I was getting an adrenaline rush in anticipation

I'll never forget the way you looked

    and how my knees got weak,

And how my hands couldn't wait to wrap around you.

A.K.

She dances effortlessly,

      like the music is coming from inside her.

A.K.

Notes on Hobby

Write a poem, a short story, or even draw your favorite hobby.
Tag @_keep_writing on Instagram and use the hashtags #Magic-
ForAlina and #MyHobby

Date a person that makes you laugh,

Who will make a complete fool out of themselves,

Just to hear your giggle

And then tickle you and cover you with kisses

Date that person.

A.K.

Romeo and Juliet's infamous balcony in Verona, Italy.

I think about you all the time

    At home, at work, in the car, in the gym, at the supermarket, while I'm hanging out with my friends

    My mind automatically comes back to you.

A.K.

Be with someone who puts your brain
in overdrive.

A.K.

She's a wild child

She's a lady

She's a honey

She's a little crazy

She loves with all her heart

She keeps her head up high

Don't try to get in her way

But cheer her by her side.

A.K.

NOTES ON BEING POWERFUL

Write a poem, a short story, or even draw something that makes you feel powerful. Tag @_keep_writing on Instagram and use the hashtags #MagicForAlina and #Powerful

Another photo from Alina's last photoshoot before she lost her hair.

Nothing shines brighter
Than a happy girl.

A.K.

NOTES ON TRUE-SHINE

Write a poem, a short story, or even draw someone that makes you shine. Tag @_keep_writing on Instagram and use the hashtags #MagicForAlina and #Shine

Alina with her best friend Deylis in Vail, Colorado.

I miss you
There, I admit it
I miss you
Day and night
I miss you.

A.K.

I LOVE rainy days,

I just don't like rainy weeks.

A.K.

When she stopped dreaming in colors,

She knew she was in real trouble.

A.K.

"You want to see magic?" she said
Stretching out her arm in front of her
  "Touch my arm"
As he circled her wrist with his fingers,
he saw goosebumps go up her whole arm
  "Magic," she whispered.

A.K

Notes on First Love

Write a poem, a short story, or even draw your first love. Tag @_keep_writing on Instagram and use the hashtags #MagicForAlina and #FirstLove

While she was staring at the moon
And the stars,
he was staring at her.

A.K.

Don't forget to enjoy the sunrises
And the sunsets

The beginnings are as beautiful
As the end.

A.K.

Alina adored her rednose pitbull Leia.

Dedicated to Leia

We fight over the blanket

And when you take the whole bed

When you steal my pillow

With your gigantic head…

Leia and her sister Laika sunbathing in the sun.

You love to plop yourself on my stomach

Making me lose my air

So nonchalant and arrogant

But you just want to cuddle cuz you care…

And those hungry eyes always begging

Always staring at my food

Following my fork around

With a little drool cuz it smells so good…

Alina with her baby Leia.

You are my companion for life

    My forever pain in the butt

I love you with all my heart

    My crazy dog, my sweetest mutt.

A.K.

Notes on Your Pet

Write a poem, a short story, or even draw your pet or a favorite animal. Tag @_keep_writing on Instagram #MagicForAlina and use the hashtags #MyFurryBaby and #MyFavoriteAnimal

Alina loved drinking prosecco with her friends.

I hate the fact that I have to stop myself

    From texting you

    Staring at the blinking vertical line,

    waiting for those three dots to pop up.

               A.K.

Alina's friends and family had a lot of love for her; she was always up for an adventure, a cup of coffee and good company.

When your name pops up on my phone

It puts the biggest silliest goofiest smile

On my face.

A.K.

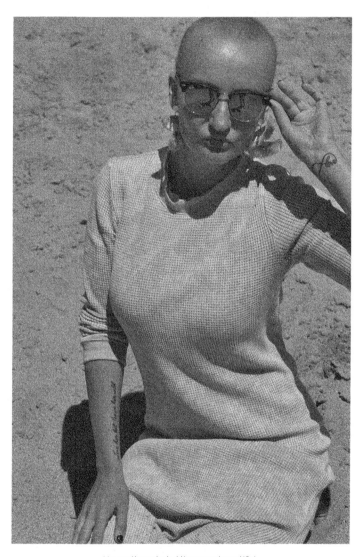

No matter what, Alina was beautiful.

She has a poker face

    And thick walls around her heart

                She's been through hell and back

       Returning stronger by being broken apart.

                          A.K.

NOTES ON COMEBACK STORY

Write a poem, a short story, or even draw your comeback story. Tag @_keep_writing on Instagram and use the hashtags #MagicForAlina and #PhoenixRising

When all you wanna do is be normal
Knowing you'll never be normal.

A.K.

A white rose from Alina's life celebration ceremony in Palm Beach, Florida.

He was her muse
But he would never know that.

A.K.

Alina loved all water sports; her childhood nickname was "mermaid." Here she is paddleboarding in the Virgin Islands.

Don't tell me to smile, make me smile.

A.K.

The final goodbye

    Was not my fault

In just one night

    You turned our love into a fraud.

A.K.

NOTES ON BROKEN HEART

Write a poem, a short story, or even draw your idea of a broken heart or lost love. Tag @_keep_writing on Instagram and use the hashtags #MagicForAlina and #BrokenHeart

If I could go back in time
I'd do it all over again
Knowing exactly how it all ends
Just so I could feel your touch again.

A.K.

He grinned

　She smiled

　　And their lives were never the same.

A.K.

You say I can't be friends

With you

I say you can't be friends

With me

Who's wrong?

Who's right?

A.K.

Your happiness

    Is not my happiness,

My happiness

    Is not your happiness.

A.K.

Notes on Life Goals

Write a poem, a short story, or even draw your life goals. Tag @_keep_writing on Instagram and use the hashtags #MagicForAlina and #LifeGoals

Journey of Alina's Ashes

The last journey for the three musketeers: During this trip, Alina's mom and sister traveled the world to spread Alina's ashes.

SAINT-TROPEZ, FRANCE
9/16/18

PETROZAVODSK, RUSSIA
10/5/18

SANTORINI, GREECE
9/24/18

Letter From The Family

This book is published in Alina's memory. Her ultimate dream has finally come true: She always wanted to be a published author. Since she was a little girl, Alina wrote stories in her journal in Russian. When she moved to the U.S., she continued to write, this time in English. A life-altering sickness stopped Alina from finishing her books, and her family and friends have stepped in and done it for her. Thank you for all of your love and support.

We urge you to please take care of yourself. Please take the time to get physicals, annual checkups and necessary vaccines. If you experience any kind of pain, go see a doctor right away. Let our story be your warning. If Alina would've gone to a doctor much sooner, her cancer could have been treatable.

Lastly, love yourself and the people around you. We don't know what happens when people pass on, but we do know how it feels to lose a loved one, a daughter, a sister, a friend, a partner.

CREDITS

This book is a collaboration. It has been a healing process and reunited so many of us who love Alina so much and miss every single day. We thank the following people that made this book a reality:

Irina Smirnova (mom + photographer)

Zlata Kotmina (sister)

Laura Kyarova (sister, by choice)

Atticus (poet)

Lola Thelin (editor)

Andrea Huff (art director)

Samantha DeLage (the crew)

Deylis Sequeira (best friend)

Charles Schwartz

Brandon Lawrenson

David Rogers

Lola Astanova

Victor Mora

Boris Polevshchikov

Made in the USA
Middletown, DE
19 September 2019